GW01336283

Memory Forest

by

Gaynor Kane

First published 2019 by The Hedgehog Poetry Press

Published in the UK by
The Hedgehog Poetry Press
Coppack House, 5
Churchill Avenue
Clevedon
BS21 6QW

www.hedgehogpress.co.uk

ISBN: 978-1-9160908-5-9

Copyright © Gaynor Kane 2019

Cover art © Bonnie Helen Hawkins

Centre Spread pencil drawing 'Keening' © Bonnie Helen Hawkins 2019

Illustrations © Tommy McMahon

The right of Gaynor Kane to be identified as the author of this work has been asserted in accordance with the Copyright, Designs and Patents Act 1988.

All rights reserved. No part of this publication may be reproduced, stored in or introduced into a retrieval system, or transmitted in any form, or by any means (electronic, mechanical, photocopying, recording or otherwise) without prior written permissions of the publisher. Any person who does any unauthorised act in relation to this publication may be liable for criminal prosecution and civil claims for damages,

9 8 7 6 5 4 3 2 1

A CIP Catalogue record for this book is available from the British Library.

For My Parents

Contents

After life	7
The Paddle Out	8
Sum wish upon a star	9
The Tree Seed Pod	10
Leave the mirrors be	11
The Low Country Farmer	12
The Low Country Farmer	13
Bury me – under *Google* search results	14
Tradition	15
I'd like to be awake for my wake	17
Varanasi	18
Keening	19
Last Walk in the Forest	20
The Long Barrow	24
Cinders	27
The List	28
Burial Beads	30
Don't waste money on me	31
Famadihana	32
Mummy left us	35
I'm a record, baby!	36
Pre-planned	37
Saṃsāra	38
North Sea Discovery	39
NOTES	41
Acknowledgments	42

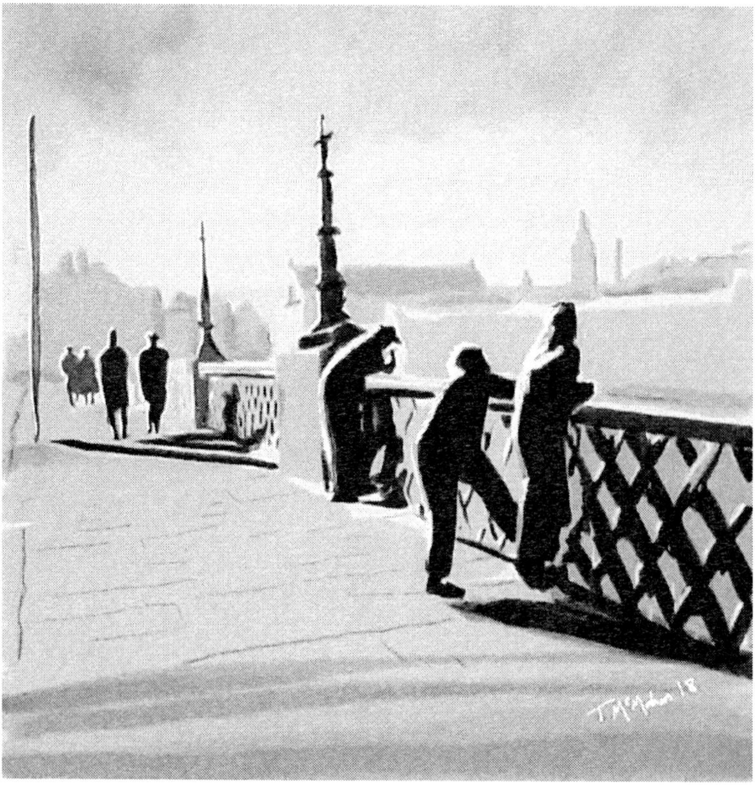

AFTER LIFE

Build me a Viking longship
symmetrical shallow hull,
oak clinker, iron rivets,
fiery dragon figurehead.

Build a pyre, with hard wood,
scribe logs cut from old Irish
forests where storytellers
spin yarns, entwine myths.

Interlock them high, a sturdy boss.
Upon this titanic target lay me out
with sword, shield, and harp;
slipper my feet in wolfhound.

Sail my ship into Belfast Lough
at the foot of the holy mountain.
Line up an artillery of archers
to shoot six ends from self-crafted bows.

Watch flaming arrows fishtail
across an obsidian sky.
Burning boat will begin
my voyage to Odin.

THE PADDLE OUT

We paddle out
in shorts and ties,
waxed sticks slide
over an unbearably blue sea.
Flat, no froth, not even
a single bubble;
the waves are
mourning too.

Our boards converge
in a circle like sunrays.
Or the many hands
of a friendship clock.
We let our thoughts
settle on him.
Resist resenting the wave
he hit like a wall.

We frisbee flower-garlands;
they overlap in Olympic rings.

SUM WISH UPON A STAR

I won't go to Heaven:
I can't believe it exists above a world
in which the Church is corrupt
and priests refuse
to apologise.

I will be astral, celestial,
incandescent.
People will be guided
from A to B
across seas
by me.

Look closely
at the night sky
and you will see
me calculating calculus
with cardinal numbers;
correlating changing values.

THE TREE SEED POD

I died, took back my foetal form, returned to an egg. My nutrients enriched soil, fed the seed planted on me. I grew two leaves, then my stem broke earth and I felt sun like the very first time.

Slowly, it happened so slowly, I was fragile for years, encased in a protective tube. Breeze made me bend, strengthened my trunk. Now, my grandchildren bring their children to my memory forest, picnic under sacred shade, teach all the species' names, tell the tale of my metamorphoses. I get hugs.

often called a tree-hugger
now I'm Daphne encapsulated
in an Ash tree.

LEAVE THE MIRRORS BE

watch me sleep
knowing that I will
not get trapped
in the reflective portal.
I will be dreaming
of rosaries
and Our Fathers
and His will in Heaven
and you.

And you will
be drinking tea,
only tea,
and talking about me
telling tales
of an imaginary shop.

THE LOW COUNTRY FARMER

Dinnae furget tae harvest the prootas.
Put guid oil in the trekter
Oul Tam fra doon the loanen
isnae alood tae plew m'fiels.
I'll spin in ma grave
if ye sell ma grun.

Bid fareweel til the donkey
fur he's a richt cliver yin,
gae up til him an stroke his cheek
(he likes thon)
whusper in his ear that I'm awa
and wullnae be bringin carrots ony mair.
Luk intil his een
watch fer the nod.
He was ma fav'rite.

THE LOW COUNTRY FARMER

Do not forget to harvest the potatoes.
Put good oil in the tractor.
Old Tom from down the lane
is not allowed to plough my fields.
I will spin in my grave
if you sell my land.

Say goodbye to the donkey
because he is very clever,
go up to him and stroke his cheek
(he likes that)
whisper in his ear that I am away
and will not be bringing carrots anymore.
Look into his eyes
watch for the nod.
He was my favourite.

BURY ME – UNDER *GOOGLE* SEARCH RESULTS

bury me in my boots where I fall
bury me low (with soul) out on the lone prairie
bury me high on a mountain, in my overalls
bury me standing (in smoke) at the crossroads to the West
bury me deep in the greenwood 'til I confess
bury me smiling under the sun, at wounded knee
bury me upside down (with my guns on) at make-out creek
bury me beneath the willow, in black
bury me under the red hand, with my money, with my ice
bury me alive (face down) by the river
bury me in a y-shaped coffin
bury me under the sea
bury me in the sand
bury me an angel, my love
bury me pretty – with all the lights out
bury me in satin
bury me next to you
a man will be buried treasure

TRADITION

A whitewashed cottage holds the family tight,
him — all boxed in oak and brass,
and the priest — who'd visited often that final week.

Everyone else spills out across the yard,
against paddock fences, down the lane
where daffodils bud, their heads bowed.

Burnished whin bushes catch the low sun.
Oil slicks ripple on pothole puddles.
Three hee-haws, long and low, cut silence.

Whinnied responses stuttered from four in hand,
drafts as dark as Guinness, their plumed
headgear like black clouds dancing.

Plaited tails, the smell of leather and Brasso,
oiled hooves shine, the clop of shoes shifting weight.
They breathe in sombre air, exhale acceptance.

Glass carriage, reflecting dark
pallbearers in top hats and tails
fit with Dickensian demeanour, gloved hands.

The procession takes the obedient pace
of cows to milking, along the long lane.
Every man takes a lift, order called by respectful nods.

Rural men, mostly farmers with dirty fingernails,
performing the graceful choreography
of a symbiotic ceremony. Cars convene

Ardkeen to Ballyphilip, to an ancient graveyard
on Windmill Hill, overlooking the mouth
of Strangford Lough, where he is laid to rest.

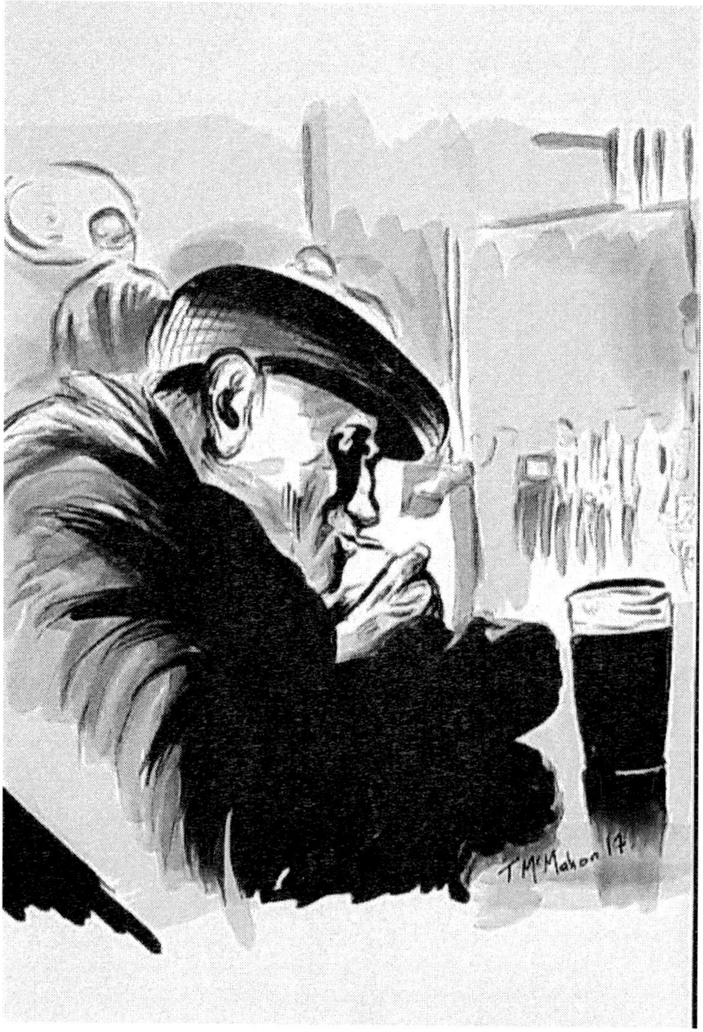
T McMahon 17

I'D LIKE TO BE AWAKE FOR MY WAKE

Here — hearing mates' stories.
Do they have the same belief —
that if you've nothing nice to say,
say nothing?

Watching the wife,
to determine if her tears
are of sorrow or relief.

At my awake
we'll sing old songs 'cause
darlin' the night is just beginning;
drink Guinness with whiskey chasers,
have a lock-in, forget to order taxis
for *that-away only leads to home.*

VARANASI

Fumes, rumble of rickshaws, motorcycles, cars.
Thousands of feet walking labyrinthine lanes.
Divine cattle amble around lowing a lament.
The pong of polluted holy river,
stench of smouldering embers.

Hotel Death, where old women wait
for the end; barred windows, bare cell,
sleep with their feet aligned north.
Awaiting life liberation
from a constant cycle of rebirth;
moksha – soul salvation.

Sandalwood smoke in their nostrils. Camphor clouds
curl from an earthen lamp held by a Hindu holy man,
with saffron smeared forehead and marigold garlands.
Incantations, drums, harmonium,
hymns, brass bells.

The desire for a ritual:
washing, white shroud,
big toes tied together,
hands palm to palm in prayer,
turmeric on forehead,
body placed on mango wood pyre
on the bank of the holy river Ganges.

KEENING

In the centre of President's Park,
she stands, arms outstretched,
cradling a taxidermic crow
in the palms of her hands;

presenting it to the world
like a sacrifice. Black wings
murder a blue sky
then weigh down

the top branches.
Deafen the dog-walkers,
joggers and chess-players
with their screeching and cawing.

They jump from branch
to branch and then,
as quick as they arrived,
fly away; respects paid.

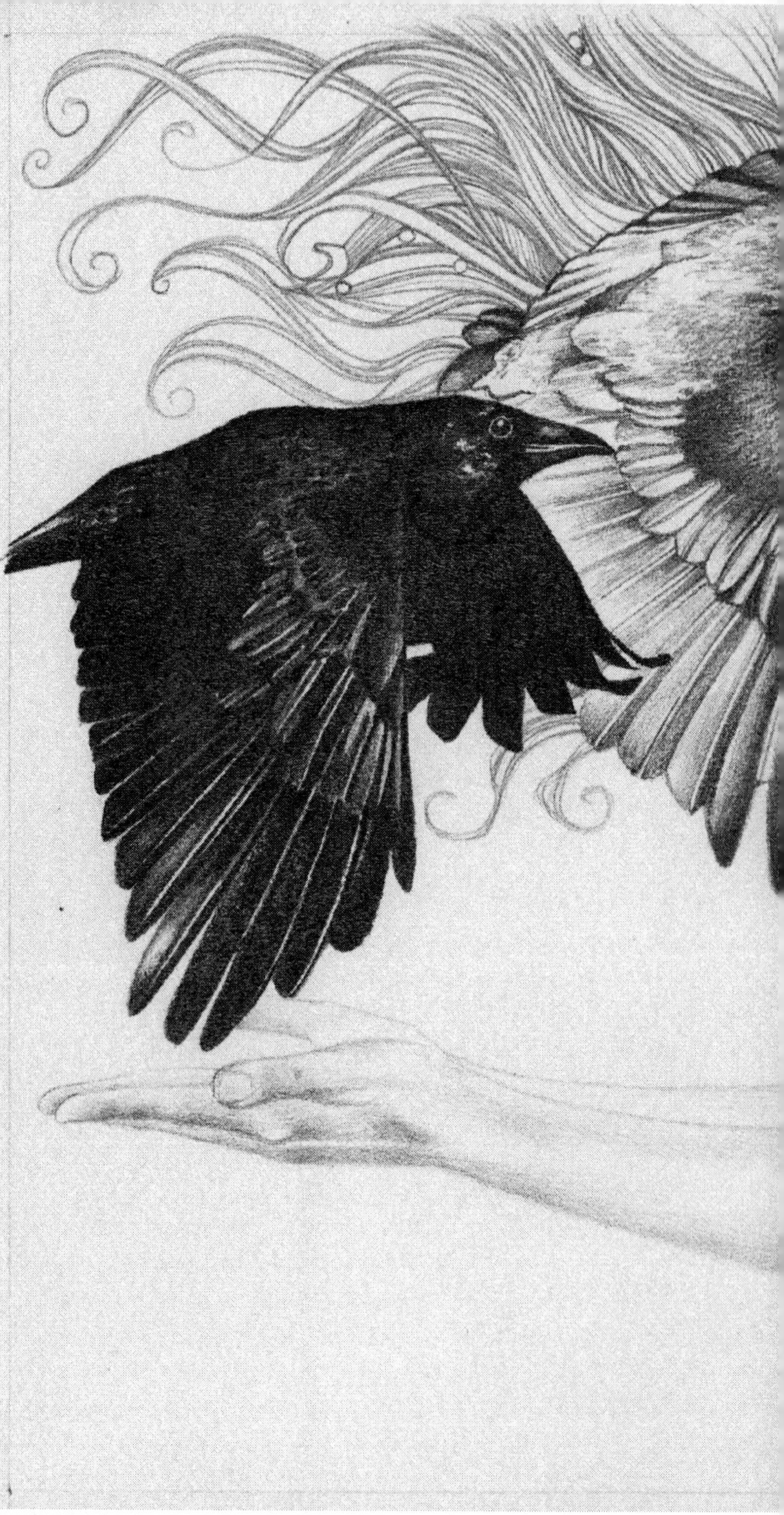

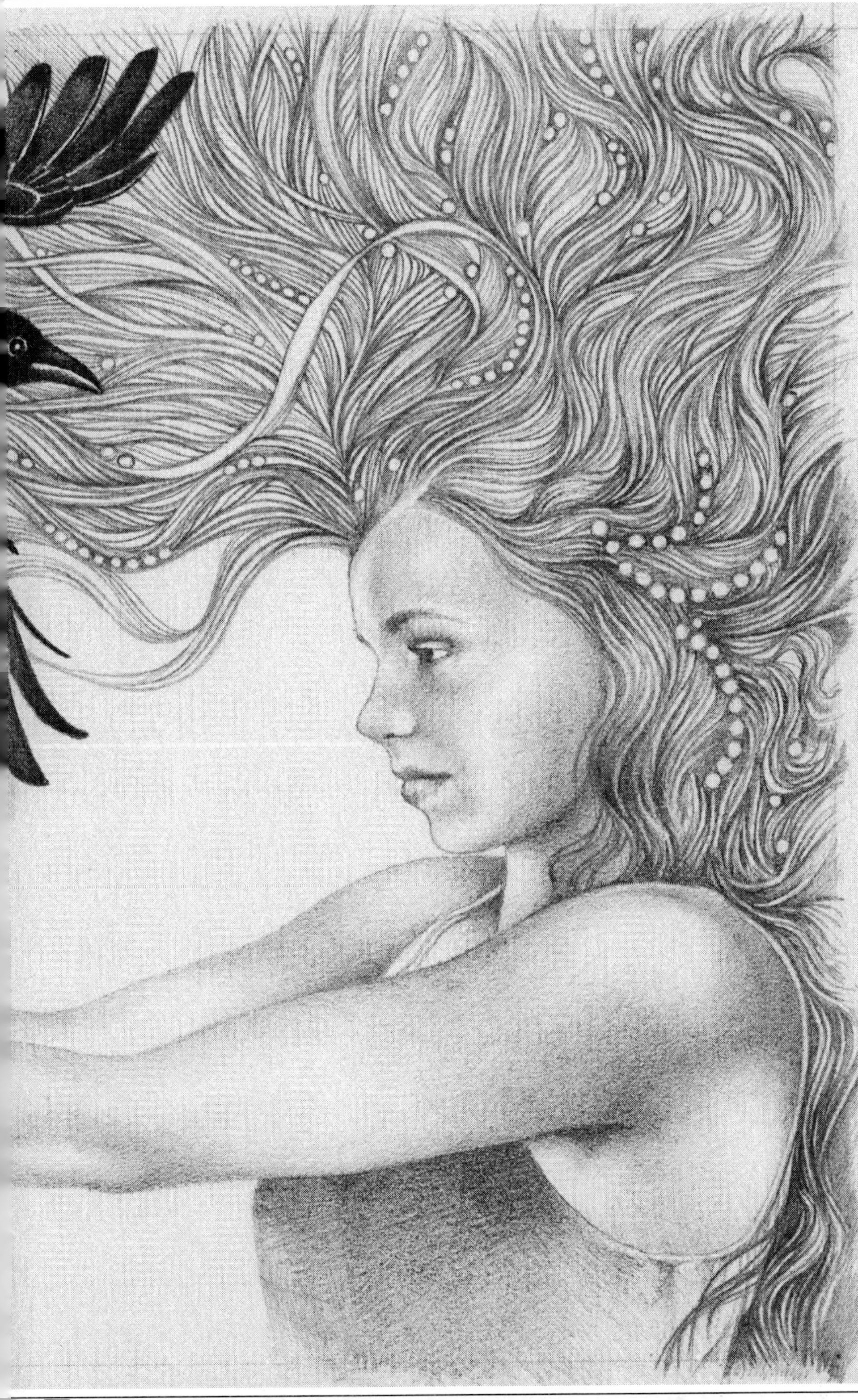

LAST WALK IN THE FOREST

I helped him up the hill. Two NHS walking sticks glinted in the light of a quickening moon. Underfoot, curling leaves crunched. We listened to a woodpecker, its Morse code tapping, telling the forest a bedtime tale. Branches brushed, twigs snapped, distant river rushed.

Past rows of tall pines casting straight-lined moon shadows. Scent of mild disinfectant. In deeper, deeper still. We stopped, him to catch his breath, me to crook my neck skywards. Above the canopy an expanse of pin-cushioned ebony sky, like shiny tacks he used in his carpentry work before his fingers bent backwards. A snowy owl swooped past, large orange eyes blinking. We felt wing-breeze on our cheeks.

Towards the middle of the forest the planting naturalised. Ahead, in a clearing, stood an ancient tree. A lightning strike had struck its higher branches. They were broken, bare and gnarled, yet it lived on. He nodded.

owl, hoot hoot hoots a
final trumpet call of God
his life on earth ending

***

At the 'Silver Surfers' he was learning to use the iPad he'd received from the kids for Christmas. He had a smart TV, to access apps and stream videos. There was one replicating a fireplace, if you watched it long enough an arm reached in from the corner of the screen to poke the logs. He used that when reading his eBooks, to give the room a cosy glow without all the hassle of the ashes.

Today, in the library, he was surfing the web. The world so small now, you could go virtually anywhere – forest graves in Sweden, native Americans building burial scaffolding in branches, the rituals across the Philippines.

hollowed out trunk
picked in person before death:
Caviteño tree burials

* * *

I returned with planks for a hut and he instructed me how to construct a simple structure. The family had put together a rota. He wouldn't be alone. Interrupting the lyrical forest soundtrack with chainsaw and chisels, we hollow out the trunk of his big tree. He must have known it would only be a few days. Shuffling, blackthorns replacing crutches, scrapping the leafy floor, he went from hut to hollowed tree trunk.

Pulled back the bark door behind himself. We sealed him in.

gifted oxygen
give myself back to the tree
a life endowment

THE LONG BARROW

Over ritual Sunday papers
you read me the story:
A modern day megalithic
burial chamber crouching
within Wiltshire lay lines,
from Avebury to Stonehenge.
Passage tomb, five chambers,
beehive domed rooves,
cobblestone concentric cocoons.

You said you'd like to walk
the passageway, bathed in glow
of rising Solstice sun
as frost flickered above,
on earthen tumulus.
Wished to find your niche,
select a shelf for eternity.
But Death's scythe cut you down
before you had the chance.

I'd never noticed the affinity before.
Assumed them purely decorative:
black and orange motifs
on bathroom tiles, pink and blue
appliqué on the quilt. Your clothes
and accessories had them too:
a silk fan of emerald
embroidered ethereal wings,
bronze buckle on red shoes.

But when you'd gone,
they came calling,
even when windows and doors
were closed. Gatekeepers came,
purple emperor perched on your
pillow, painted lady on the landing,
swallowtails in sitting room,
peacock on pelmet,
skippers in the kitchen.

At All Cannings, I carried you
across flat fields; pewter urn
chilling my skin.
Two large sarsen stones
stand sentry, a gate fit
for a courageous chieftain,
threshold between
the land of the living
and the land of the dead.

Walking the dim passage,
to pick your spot,
I found a butterfly
resting on a ledge
and knew
you'd found your niche.

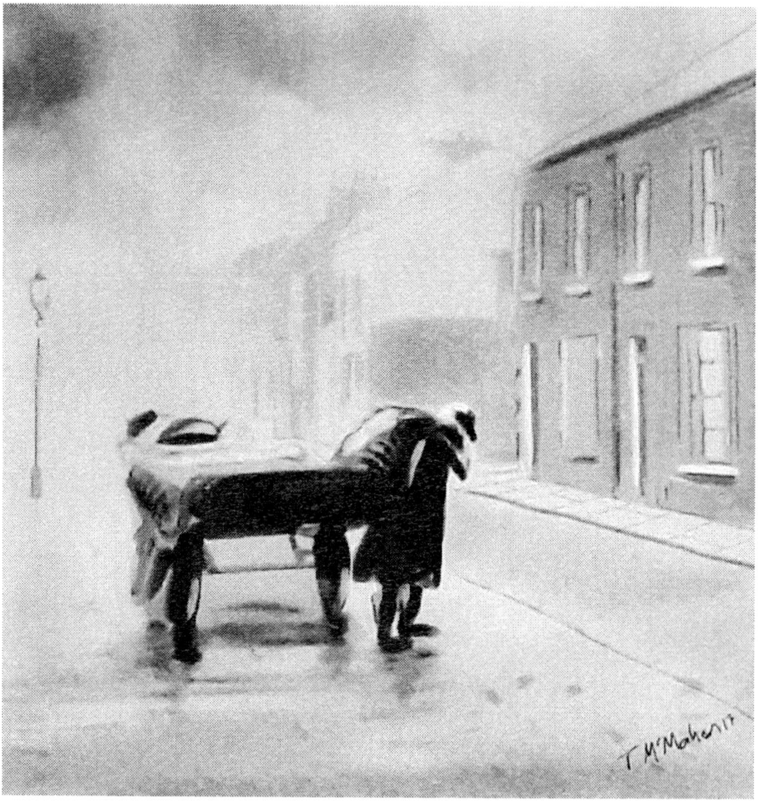

CINDERS

As a wee'n I ate mortar
scraped from joints
between Belfast brick.
I crunched coal.
Collected lollipop sticks,
pieces of paper
and thrown-away-things.
In the alley I made fire,
lit by safety match.

So, this firebug is happy
to go up in flames
all I ask,
is that as the coffin
descends to the retort,
you play
The Final Countdown.

THE LIST

Jaundiced and blotched
with champagne spray
from her fiftieth party
the list remains
stuck to the fridge
by a Greek magnet
with its white church,
round med-blue roof,
Aegean Sea and island background.

Her thirst for rockrose gin and languages;
asking the ouzeri owner
if there was a word for island-hopping.
Always told travellers to avoid
the tourist trilogy –
Delos, Mykonos, Santorini.

Written before the gallbladder op,
just in case, eighty/twenty good odds
but there's always a risk;
It stayed there after,
while she painted
roses through recovery.

Island cliffs, white flowers
(one would bloom each day)
to signify protection.
She laboured over
cliff roses' shredded bark.
Perfected the pinks and purples of Cistus.

Amber perfume and gin
are listed, below
a spray of bright bougainvillea
like those trimming the alleyways
and arches of Paros.

Confession at the Church
of one hundred doors,
tracing Byron's signature,
awe of spiral stalagmites,
stolen kisses in the Chamber
of the Stone Waterfall.

Bread and honey
Homer honey from Ios
where beehives dot the valley of his burial,
guarded by a sentinel
of three white chapels,
the birthplace of the Iliad and the Odyssey.
Old men sit under ancient oaks
playing backgammon,
hatted against dry winds.

List the hymns:
All Things Bright and Beautiful,
Jerusalem and *Rock of Ages*.
A song written in a storm,
composer took shelter
under a rocky outcrop.

Remained a fridge relic after.
She, at the kitchen-table
planning our next adventure.

Like the Etesian wind,
her heart-attack
blew in unexpectedly
and took her breath away.

BURIAL BEADS

Millions of years ago in a prehistoric forest
a praying mantis landed on bark, perhaps
she stood too still before attacking her prey,
was engulfed within a golden globe.

Gold-leaf tear of demise; now honeyed amber
perfectly preserves her. Genuflecting; begging gods
to show lost cave dwellers their way home.
Egyptians thought the 'bird-fly' led souls

to the underworld and bees were birthed
from sun gods' tears. Against the background
of a fiery dawn, reflected in hazel highlights
of your eyes; I'm reminded of the amber

breasted kingfisher, skimming the Corrib,
during our annual pilgrimage West. Shimmering
feathers of cerulean, electric, sapphire; flying
through rainbowed spray of rushing waters below.

Sapphire is my birthstone,
precious blue. Burn me into beads
of coloured liquid light;
like the rough gem you say I am.

DON'T WASTE MONEY ON ME

buy yourself a TV -
remember evenings we shared
watching films and eating popcorn.

Don't -
        TVs are all slimline
        that won't do
        buy a sofa,
        a big, soft, comfy, sofa
        in a box.

Bury me in the box,
        no fancy mahogany coffin
        or costly compostable casket.

Play music:
        Metal;
        AMPLIFIED.

FAMADIHANA

Six years, three hundred and sixty-four days
since we laid the long wreath of white lilies,
roses and spray carnations on mound of soil,
dropped handfuls of claggy clay into grave,
watched it break into lumps on hitting oak lid,
tea and sandwiches in the working men's club after.

Veronique went to Lidl for wine,
cheap stuff would be fine. There was an offer
on party prosecco. Hamilton took to B&Q
for shovels. I cleared the airing cupboard
of old sheets. Yellowing linen; perfect.

We have no idea where you had heard
about it or why you would ask
for it to be done. The solicitor
didn't know where to look
when she read out the will.
You are turning
us into lawbreakers.

Belfast City Council
has no policy
for dancing with the dead.

On the night of the seventh anniversary
we exhume your coffin,
thankful that your plot
is far enough back from the road.
How strange
a sight it would be
for folk on the Glider
or ambulance drivers
returning to hospital.

We light scores of pillar candles. Purple-gloved,
we lift out your fossil form, swaddle you
in sheets, sprayed with scent of rosé wine.
Play *I Wanna Dance With Somebody*
on your old ghetto-blaster and dance
around the plot, conga style.

Popping prosecco, we offer you a drink.
Sign our names on the sheet with black marker;
all the family, including those not with us
and two tiny tots you never met.

Under a haloed mourning moon,
we join hands knowing that
everyone in the world
sees their own version.
We say the Lord's prayer

and turn your bones.

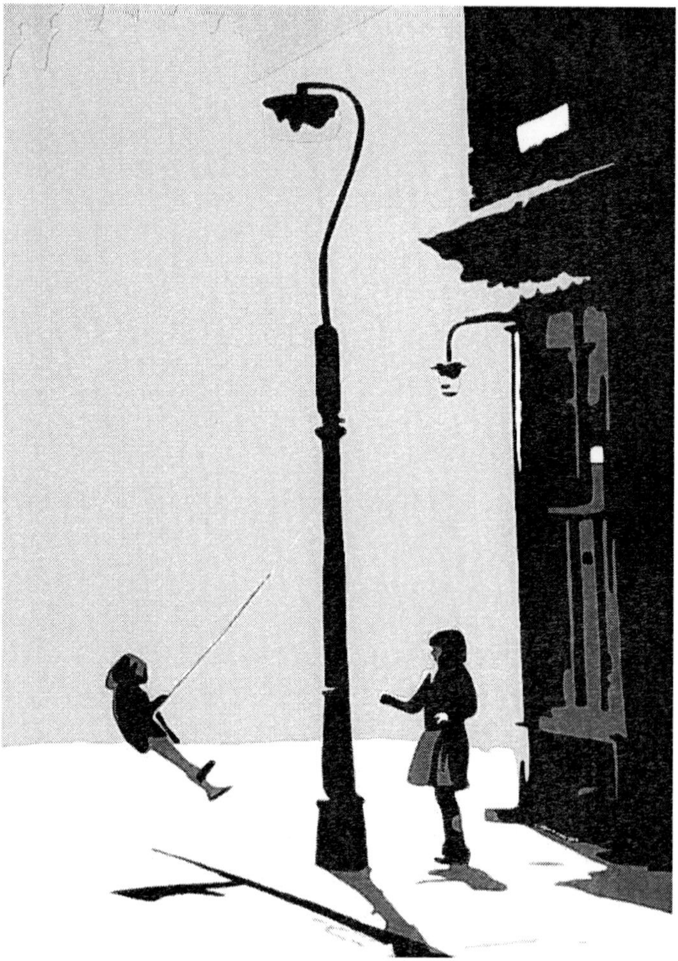

MUMMY LEFT US

a video, she'd had Dad put lipstick on her
and eyeshadow and mascara.
The sun was shining, she looked
like an angel wearing a mask.

She told us she loved us
like she had every day
for four months
and that she would always be guiding us.

We shouldn't be sad or sorry
for she was in a better place now.
We wondered how that could be.
I think she meant she was pain-free.

We were to arrange her party
wear bright colours, tell stories,
read poems, play music
to celebrate her life.

We decided to have rainbow cake,
blow bubbles, wear wings, tiaras and tutus.
Dad helped organise an adult-sized
slip 'n' slide and bouncy castle.

Mummy would've enjoyed her party.

I'M A RECORD, BABY!

I've always dreamed
of making a record.
Single, extended play,
album, airplay, charts,
or platinum, didn't matter.

Took two days in a studio
to lay down some tracks.
Dictated the family tree,
wove latticework branches.
Audio anecdotes, quotes;
recited poetry, lines.

End-of-life industry,
a growing market;
I saw the tin stamp made,
hills and mountains
for words and notes
in concentric circles.

Picked clear wax
for the biscuits.
This'll be a low volume run
but it will be no white label;
colour photo in the centre.

My cremains will glitter
on vinyl like fool's gold.
They'll add a lot of fizz,
crackle, scratch and pop.
My MP3 file in the grooves.

PRE-PLANNED

Go to the Co-Op,
find my coffin chosen,
funeral paid for.
Order only one wreath;
lilies forbidden.

Decide whether to bury or cremate.
I can't work out which is worse;
decomposing and devoured by worms;
or being sent to the furnace alive.

During a nice church service, sing
Make me a channel of your peace.
Or better still,
have Daniel O'Donnell do it.

SAMSĀRA

Freckles, age spots on hands like stains
of bridal body ink. Eggshell skin, delicate
as Sanjhi paper art, creased tissue.

* * *

I fly over a stream of consciousness,
become reborn a Demoiselle,
in northern nesting grounds.

Long neck, a compass point
on a hardwired migration path.
Flocks rising heavenwards,
raptures of satin ribbons,
ascend over mountains of oblivion,
to a desert plain of existence.
Our lungs exalted, fortified to reach
Himalayan heights, where air is thin.

My silhouette, love's messenger in reflexion.
My dance, a sedge of sacred steps.
My wingspan, the sound of a thousand breaths.
My eyes, two drops of past-life-blood in the yolk.

Each year, the perilous pilgrimage to Khichen;
welcomed with grain, protected from predators.
Praised.

Coupled in a continuous cycle. Laying
henna speckled eggs. Forgetting
what was once written on skin.

NORTH SEA DISCOVERY

Murky, cold, almost baltic. The divers'
submersible lights converge; x marking the spot.

An outline, a man becoming an island,
colonies of corals circled by wolf fish, red fish, ling.

Anchored feet on rubble of dead reef,
a sloping seabed in an iceberg ploughmark;

nutrient rich flesh and swelling undercurrent,
perfect for encouraging *Lophelia Pertusa*.

Living reef, growing, budding, flowering
on death warmed up by flame shells.

Orange gorgonians in orifices, horny skeleton finger
fan anemones, golden sponges on skull like hair buns.

The aquanauts wonder who he is, what he has been,
then realise it no longer matters;

he has created a universe – sunfish, stars, asteroids,
a big bang of pink and purple fireworks.

NOTES

Samsāra – is a Sanskrit word meaning wandering and is also a doctrine of some religions, such as Buddhism.

The Low Country – is the colloquial name for the Ards Peninsula (situated on Northern Ireland's East coast). The poem is written in the vernacular of that area with input from local man, Mark Thompson.

The List – was inspired by Sandra who holidays in Greece and once asked asked if there was a Greek word for island-hopping.

Keening – was written in response to an article stating that crows are the latest added to the group of animals known to recognise, or even mourn, following research by the University of Washington.

Burial Beads – a practice popular in Korea involving heat and the compression of ashes into gem-like beads in different colours.

The Long Barrow – was written in response to an article on the BBC news website about a modern-day long barrow (tomb) being opened in Wiltshire, England and the first paying customer.

Famadihana – the turning of the bones. A tradition of the Malagasy people of Madagascar during which they exhume the bodies of loved one, wrap them in cloth and dance.

ACKNOWLEDGMENTS

Appreciative acknowledgement is made to the editors of the following publications, in which some of these poems appeared: Sixteen Magazine, The Curlew, and The Selkie.

I'm indebted to Holywood Writer's Group for their constant support and considered critique (particularly Robert, Sandra and Veronika for close readings of this collection).

Much gratitude to the Irish Writers' Centre for their mentoring scheme and Mary Montague for her valuable feedback on some of the poems.

Thanks to Bonnie Helen Hawkins for the cover image 'November Light' and granting permission to publish the drawing that so beautifully illustrated my poem 'Keening' when included in her 52 Crows Project.

Thanks also to poets Mary Montague, Sue Burge, Isabelle Kenyon and Colin Dardis for their endorsements.

I thank Mark Davidson for his belief in me and good humour. He is a joy to work with.

I'm grateful for the enduring support of my family and friends; many of whom, were the inspiration for these poems.